Guinea Pigs
A Practical Treatise on their Breeding, Feeding and Management of Cavies

by *Walter E. Clarke*

with an introduction by Jackson Chambers

Self Reliance Books

Get more historic titles on animal and stock breeding, gardening and old fashioned skills by visiting us at:

http://selfreliancebooks.blogspot.com/

Introduction

I am pleased to present yet another title in the "Cavies" series.

The work is in the Public Domain and is re-printed here in accordance with Federal Laws.

Though this work is a century old it contains much information on bees that is still pertinent today.

As with all reprinted books of this age that are intended to perfectly reproduce the original edition, considerable pains and effort had to be undertaken to correct fading and sometimes outright damage to existing proofs of this title. At times, this task is quite monumental, requiring an almost total "rebuilding" of some pages from digital proofs of multiple copies. Despite this, imperfections still sometimes exist in the final proof and may detract from the visual appearance of the text.

I hope you enjoy reading this book as much as I enjoyed making it available to readers again.

Jackson Chambers

CONTENTS.

ILLUSTRATIONS

GUINEA PIGS

CHAPTER I.

GENERAL INFORMATION.

The Guinea Pig is a little animal of the rabbit family. It is not a pig at all, and just why it is called "Guinea Pig" nobody seems to know. It is in no sense a pig, and it did not originate in Guinea. In shape it does not resemble the pig as much as it resembles a squirrel or a rabbit. The proper name of the animal is Cavy, although it is seldom known, in the United States at'least, by any other name than Guinea Pig. The writer uses both names indiscriminately.

The animal is wholly vegetarian, and eats about the same foods as the rabbit. The fur of the smooth-haired cavy is of a texture similar to the fur of the rabbit. When "dressed" for cooking it resembles the squirrel, except that the full-grown cavy is larger, weighing between two and three pounds.

Most Easily Raised.

The Cavy or Guinea Pig has the important distinction of being more easily raised than any other animal, owing to the facts that it is practically exempt from disease and that it can be successfully raised in smaller quarters in proportion to its size than any other animal. It is thoroughly domesticated, having been raised in captivity for some centuries.

It originated in South America, and at the time when that country was first explored and settled by the Spaniards the cavy was one of the principal domestic animals then raised for food. The Indians raised them in great numbers and kept them in their huts. There are also some wild varieties, which are hunted as game in certain parts of South America. When properly cooked in any of the many different ways, the cavy is as delicious as any meat could be. The United States Government recommends the raising of cavies for food because of the facts that but little space, small capital and only ordinary knowledge are required; the animals are very hardy, easily managed, may be successfully reared in any locality, and the demand is rapidly increasing, thus insuring a ready market at remunerative prices.

Description.

Our illustrations are drawn by Mr. E. G. Lutz, an artist whose work as a portrayer of animal life is well known, and his pictures give a better idea of the animals than any written description could. Cavies have rather short, stocky bodies, short legs, heads somewhat like a rabbit, but the ears are very small; there are four toes on the front feet and three on the hind feet; the fur may be almost any color, and there are short, smooth-haired, rough-haired and long-haired varieties.

Demand for Cavies.

Cavies are not well known in the United States, consequently there is at present but little or no demand for them for food; but there is a good demand for them as pets and for laboratory uses. A Government report says: "Laboratories now report that suitable stock is scarce, and that they have been paying from $1.00 to $1.50 for their supply of young animals." The same

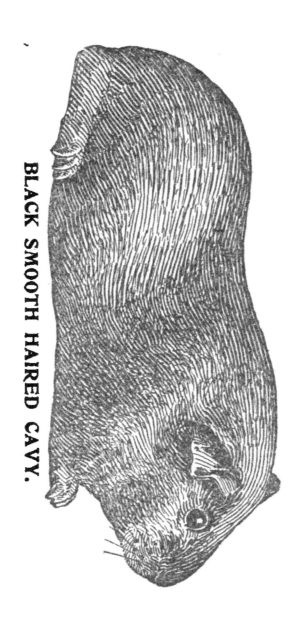

BLACK SMOOTH HAIRED CAVY.

report says that the Government has raised guinea pigs to maturity (4 or 5 months) at a cost of 50 to 60 cents, and that private breeders with their own labor, especially those with plenty of green food at command, could probably reduce the cost by half. The laboratories prefer the young animals of about six weeks old.

Cavy Farms.

Cavy raising is a new industry in the United States, but already there are a number of Cavy farms, where the little animals are raised in considerable quantities, and on some of these farms a careful and correct pedigree is kept of all of the best specimens. Many persons who have failed to make a success of poultry have converted their hen houses into caviaries, and are now doing with the animals that which they never could do with the birds: making money. They find the Cavies require less care and are not subject to so many ailments as the poultry was troubled with. There are no incubators or brooders to watch. The Cavies require no artificial heat; merely a dry, windproof house, with hay or straw for bedding.

CHAPTER II.

VARIETIES.

The common guinea pig, the kind usually raised in America for pets, for experiments in breeding, for laboratory use or for food, is the smooth-haired variety—or mixture of many varieties—and may be of almost any color, but most frequently is spotted with two or more colors. They may be black, white, red, cream, chocolate or fawn, and sometimes a single specimen will have a generous mixture of colors. If we select and breed a well-matched pair of this sort it is by no means certain or even likely that their youngsters will show any marked resemblance to the parents. By breeding the same doe to another buck of similar markings we may get a litter entirely different from the first lot. It must be understood, however, that from a lot of common guinea pigs we may, by careful breeding, produce in the course of a short time any particular color or marking desired; that is, anything within the limits of the ancestors. For example, suppose we have an assorted lot of cavies and want to raise all white ones.

We would select say one buck, the one with the most white in his coat, and breed with him the two whitest does. When the young females are sufficiently matured breed the whitest of them to their sire. Breed the whitest young male with the two original dams. Continue this line of breeding, and you will eventually get the color you are after, and in time can always depend on their continuing to breed that color.

Fancy Varieties.

The fancy varieties of smooth cavies are black, white, cream, red, chocolate, cinnamon, each of a single solid color; tortoise shell, brindle and many other colors, with other varieties being developed frequently. Then there are the Dutch Marked, which is a mixture of two colors, as red and white, black and white, etc., the white covering the nose, forehead, shoulders, forward part of body and the feet. The tortoise shell and white variety show a mixture of red and black with white. The Himalayan is all white except feet, ears and nose, which are jet black.

The Peruvian is a long-haired cavy usually of mixed colors, the color being considered of less importance than length of hair.

The Abyssinian is a long, rough-haired animal, which has the appearance of being all "ruffled up"; its hair growing in all directions, forming what are called rosettes. They are bred in various color markings.

Which Is Best?

The question, "Which variety is the best?" can only be answered in a general way. As pets, children might prefer the smooth-coated, mixed varieties. Ladies who keep cavies as pets usually select the all white or all black colored ones, and frequently the long-haired or

ABYSSINIAN CAVY.

Peruvian. The man who is a hobbyist might prefer one or more of the pedigreed varieties, the Abyssinian or Himalayan, as likely as any.

If the animals are raised for profit, and the output sold principally for laboratory use, we would recommend the mixed, smooth-haired ones. If for exhibition purposes or for sale to fancy breeders, then, of course, the stock must be pedigreed, and the greater the number of varieties kept the better, although many breeders of the "fancy" stick to one variety only, as this gives them a better chance to win with their special variety in the shows.

As may be supposed, the Peruvians and Abyssinians require more care, on account of their long coats, than do the smooth-haired animals. The long coats of the Peruvians especially demand some grooming to keep them at their best.

The different varieties are equally hardy and healthy, and all weigh about the same when fully grown.

CHAPTER III.

FEEDING.

The Guinea Pig or Cavy eats almost all kinds of vegetables, hay and grain, including lettuce, celery tops, cauliflower leaves, dandelion, apples, carrots, cow beets, rape, spinnach, cabbage leaves, turnips and turnip tops, oats, bran, cracked corn, wheat, rye, alfalfa, clover and grass. It must not be understood, however, that the animal requires all of the above, nor in fact any great number or variety of foods. On the contrary, the cavy would thrive on any one of the dry foods with any one of the green foods, and would not require any frequent change in the diet. So the cavy keeper is governed in the selection of food somewhat by accessibility and price.

Balanced Rations.

Different breeders feed in different ways, but usually the food is some sort of "balanced rations"; that is, some sort of green stuff is fed at least once a day and also some dry feed. This is all very simple, but to avoid any possible misunderstanding, let us define just what we mean by Green Food, Dry Food, Hay and Grass.

The Dry Foods are corn, wheat, oats, rye, barley and other grains, bran, middlings, flour, stale bread, hay, etc. The corn and wheat should preferably be cracked.

The term Hay is herein intended to include all the cut and dried grasses and clovers, such as timothy, blue grass, lawn grass, wild grasses, all the clovers and alfalfa. All kinds of hay are dry food.

By Grass we mean the same as hay, except that it is fresh cut and green, not dried. There are persons who do not know that hay is made by drying (or "curing") grass or clover. Grass, then, is always a green food.

Green Food means any undried fruits or vegetables, undried leaves of vegetables, grass, fresh cut green rye, wheat or oats grass, green leaves from corn stalks, dandelion, green pea pods—in short, any food with sap or juice in it.

Make it a rule to feed some one of the Dry Foods and some one of the Green Foods each day. The two foods need not be given at the same time unless you feed but once a day. Feed regularly at about the same hour or hours each day. It is a good plan to feed dry food in the morning, green food at noon and hay in the evening, but do not reverse frequently to a green food mornings and a dry food at noon.

Water Is Necessary.

In the morning is a good time to give a fresh, clean supply of water, which should always be supplied in abundance, so that the cavies will always have it before them. It is true that cavies will live without water for some time if they have plenty of vegetables and green grass or clover, but that is no reason for not supplying water at all times. A good water vessel may be made of a clean tin can and a saucer or small round pan. Punch a hole in the can one-half inch from the top, fill with water, place saucer or pan on top, and, holding the two pieces together, turn them upside down. The water will stand one-half inch deep in the saucer or pan until the can becomes empty. This arrangement will keep the water clean and will prevent the cavies from getting into it.

Different Methods.

Perhaps the best idea of proper feeding can be had by noting the methods of some of the most prominent breeders. One of them says: "I give them a breakfast of oats with some green stuff—usually carrots. At noon only green food, and at night some bran dampened with cold water enough to make it crumbly, and enough hay to last them twenty-four hours."

Another breeder says: "I feed whole oats, bran, cracked corn, hay cut into short pieces, water, roots and various greens."

Another says: "Dry oats is the best staple food, and I use plenty of hay the year round. Of course, I furnish lots of green food, and prefer carrots or freshly cut grass, but am careful to see that the grass is not wet. I never cut it until the dew is off."

And another feeds timothy hay and oats with any kind of green food obtainable.

The proprietor of one of the most extensive cavy farms in the United States, asked to explain his method of feeding, said: "In the morning we feed bran wet to a crumbly mass and also some cracked corn and oats mixed. At noon green food. At night we feed hay only, increasing the amount at the beginning of cold weather and supplying all they can use during the winter. We raise our lettuce, and always have a plentiful supply during the summer. We also use a great deal of green grass during the season. We raise several tons of carrots and mangles each year for green food in the winter."

Keep Dry.

An important point in the care of cavies is to keep them dry. Never feed any grass or other greens while wet or damp. Do not spill water in hutch or pen. Bear in mind that dampness will injure the health of cavies more than anything else that is likely to occur. A piece of rock salt should always be kept in the hutch.

Introducing New Foods.

When beginning to feed a new food, start with a small quantity, and gradually increase with each meal until the proper amount is reached.

Feed sparingly of cabbage, turnips and potatoes. Some breeders say these vegetables are not suitable for cavies at all, but we know of many breeders who use them in small quantities and consider them good food.

The Cavy's Choice.

If allowed to choose its food, the cavy would probably select grass in preference to any other, and they may be allowed to eat their fill of it. The grass should be clean and gathered from a place not contaminated by cats or other animals. Alfalfa is one of the best of the "grasses," and when served fresh this succulent clover is greedily eaten. It is becoming quite common, and is obtainable in nearly all parts of the United States. Never use musty hay or inferior foods of any kind.

Bread and milk are relished by cavies after they once become accustomed to it. Like most other animals, they rarely show much liking for any new food; one they have not previously had. It will be found that the cavy will flourish and be happy with almost any good food, and does not require much variety.

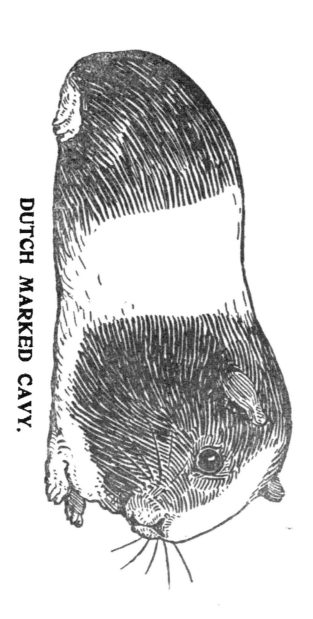

DUTCH MARKED CAVY.

CHAPTER IV.

——

BREEDING.

In the first place, let us say there Is no animal so easily bred and reared as the guinea pig (cavy). They are prolific, easily managed and practically free from ailments or disease. They are lively and clean, eat common, cheap vegetable foods, such as oats, carrots, cow beets, grass and hay. It is surprising what a quantity of hay or alfalfa they will clean up. The young are born fully furred, have their eyes open, and are able to run about at once. They do not require much room, having been domesticated for centuries, and a fence 12 inches high is sufficient to confine them. Where they are raised in great quantities and kept in separate runs it is easy for the attendant to step from one run to another without opening or closing any gate. Contrast this feature with the fences required for poultry, where some of the stock, Leghorns in particular, will fly over an eight-foot fence. Cavies are never wild or vicious, and can be handled by children without any fear of their biting or scratching. They do not burrow in the ground nor knaw through enclosures.

Selecting Stock.

Of course, if we are going to breed cavies we must first obtain some breeding stock, and this first step is really the most important of all. Let us not consider the cost of these first animals, for they are to be the parents of all we raise in the future, the source from which may spring hundreds or thousands of animals. Get good stock to start with. Get the best you can find anywhere. The best will not cost much, and to save a few dollars by starting with poor stock would be poor economy, indeed. Get good, healthy stock, that will mature quickly and grow to a good size.

Number Required.

The number of animals to be purchased will depend on how extensively we plan to go into the raising of the animals, but one buck to four does is about the right proportion. It will facilitate matters, however, to add one or two more bucks in about six months. These should be procured, if possible, from the same stock as the original. Introducing "new blood" is not at all necessary, nor is it desirable, provided the original stock was good, strong and vigorous. The need of additional bucks comes about in this way: the first young are ready to breed when six months old, but it is not wise to breed two cavies of that age together. One of them should be older. We can breed the six months' old males to their dams and the six months' old females to their sire, but at this period we should have probably 7 or 8 young females and an equal number of young males, so that we will need at least one more fully matured male.

Frequent Littering.

The period of gestation is 65 to 70 days, so that as many as five litters may be had each year from each female, but it is decidedly better to restrict the breeding to one litter every three months, and many breeders allow only two or three litters per year, as too rapid breeding produces less desirable animals. The female's first litter usually numbers only one to three young, but subsequently they will average three or four, so that, allowing four litters per year should give 12 to 15 young from each female. Now, while one buck is enough for four does, the ideal number to *start* with is one buck for every two does. For our illustration let us start with one buck and two does. We will first construct a hutch, something like those described in the chapter on Hutches.

Place the hutch in a barn or any other weather-proof building where it will be dry. Put the three guinea pigs in hutch and throw in a liberal amount of hay. Feed according to advice in Chapter III.

Line Breeding.

In about 65 to 70 days the two does should produce litters of young. When the young are born it will be well to put the buck in a separate hutch. The young will be weaned in about three weeks, and when they are 25 days old they should be removed from the does and the young males placed in one hutch and the young females in another. These young cavies will hereafter be referred to as Litter No. 1. The old buck may now be put in the hutch with the two old does. When the next litters appear you must again remove the buck, and in 25 days you will place the young of this litter No. 2 in other hutches, keeping the males and females separate. Then, having removed these last young, you may now put the females of the Litter No. 1 with their sire and put the best buck of the Litter No. 1 with the old does.

From the hutch containing the two old Does and the Buck from Litter No. 1 we will get Litter No. 3, and from the old Buck and the females from Litter No. 1 we get what we will call Litter No. 4.

When Litters Nos. 3 and 4 are six months old we may breed the females of No. 3 with males of No. 4, and the females of No. 4 with the males of No. 3, but it would be wiser to breed these six months' old cavies with older stock. Put the old Buck with three or four of these six months' old Does and the other Does of that age with Bucks of your No. 1 litter. The males of these No. 3 and 4 litters should be bred with the original old Does and with Does of Litter No. 1 and No. 2.

All this is really more simple than it may appear. It only means that you keep track of your stock, so you will know which is which, and that you observe these three rules: First—Do not breed any cavy until it is six months old. Second—Do not breed a six months' old Buck with a six months' old Doe; one of the pair should be a year or more of age. Always try to breed the youngest with the oldest. Third—Do not breed full brother and sister together.

The "Easiest Way."

An easier way, and one almost as successful where no fancy or exhibition specimens are sought, is to let old and young, male and female, all run together in one large pen, which is supplied with numerous boxes and shelves for sleeping quarters. This method is not as bad as it looks, especially where some hundreds are in the same enclosure. It will be found that the young will usually breed with the more matured, and that, as a rule, they do not breed with those closely related. The method has much to recommend it; the labor of feeding is reduced to a minimum; owing to their number the cavies can better withstand severe winter weather, and it facilitates the selection of those to be marketed. There is the objection that the young breed too early. This might be overcome by removing all young before they are one month old, and keeping the young males in one pen and the females in another. They could be replaced in the big pen as they matured.

Breeding On a Large Scale.

We know of one farm where cavies are raised in great number, both "fancy" and "utility," and are kept in pens which were originally built for brooding chicks. The cavies have proven so much more profitable that this brooder house, some hundreds of feet in length, has been turned into a cavy house. The steam pipes have been removed, as has also the poultry netting which divided the house into pens. The pens as originally built were separated with 12-inch boards, and these were left in place, so that as now in use the house is divided into pens 4 x 12 feet, with a window in each and a little sliding door, which allows the cavies to run outside in warm weather. These outside runs are separated by a small mesh wire netting which forms a fence 12 inches high. For the convenience of the attendant in feeding, etc., there is inside the building an unobstructed passageway 4 feet wide, running the entire length of the building. The fancy or exhibition stock is kept in smaller hutches and very carefully bred, but in each of these pens they keep about 50 cavies. The young are removed when a month old, the sexes separated and placed in pens with other young of about the same age. As they have several pens of young, it is quite an easy matter in this way to avoid too close inbreeding. They put the young from pens 1, 2, 3, 4, when they are weaned, into two pens, the males in Pen No. 11 and females in Pen No. 12. The young born in Pens 5, 6, 7, 8 are divided in the same way, and males put in Pen No. 13 and females in No. 14. The young from Pens 1, 2, 3, 4 are, when six months old, bred with the older animals in Pens 5, 6, 7, 8, etc. In this way the vitality of the stock is maintained at its highest, and the work of feeding and cleaning reduced to a minimum. For every 100 Does they count on an average of 4 young per day. They say the loss by death is practically nothing, as their stock is always healthy, disease being unknown. They are constantly culling out any weaklings, which they sell at a low price to a menagerie to be fed to snakes and animals. Thousands of their young cavies when about six weeks old are sent to medical colleges and laboratories, where they are used principally in testing anti-toxins and serums. This big farm also sells hundreds of cavies for pets, some of their fancy varieties bringing as high as $25.00 each, but we understand their principal revenue is derived from the many "pairs" and "pens" sold for breednig purposes.

ONE DAY OLD.

CHAPTER V.

HUTCHES.

The cavy being of all animals the easiest raised, it is not necessary that they should be kept in any particular sort of cage or building. They require clean, dry quarters, well ventilated, and in winter must be protected from cold. No artificial heat is necessary or desirable. Large numbers are frequently raised in a single room, sometimes hundreds of them, where they are given small packing boxes, usually soap boxes, in which to sleep. This method saves time in feeding and watering, but a more successful way is to have quarters so they may be separated into four lots: First—A pen for old stock, male and female. Second—A pen for females which are pregnant, or are nursing young. Third—Males under six months old. Fourth—Females under six months old.

The cut shows a very good form of hutch, manufactured and used extensively by a large breeder. It is 36

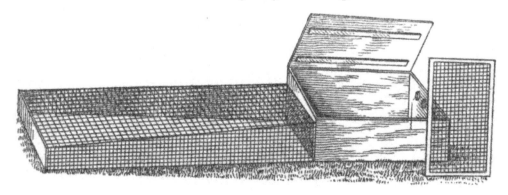

inches long, 15 inches wide and 15 inches high. A run made of wire cloth, three meshes to the inch, is attached which forms an outdoor space of 6 feet long, 15 inches wide at end next hutch and 24 inches wide at opposite end. This hutch is fitted with a shelf. One end is closed with a wire netting door, and the back end has large holes, which may be opened when additional ventilation is desired. It is weather-proof and of neat design, making it sufficiently ornamental to be used on the lawn.

Government Hutch.

The United States Bureau of Animal Industry uses a plain box 18 inches high, 20 inches wide and 42 inches long, with wire netting at each end and a shelf inside. Such a hutch accommodates a male, three or four females and the young until matured. Such hutches may be stacked up three high and thus economize room. In bad weather they must be keep indoors.

A Cheap Hutch.

A very good, inexpensive hutch may be made of a box 24 x 20 x 15 inches. Knock out one end and nail a piece of fine wire netting in its place. Do not use poultry netting, as it is too coarse. Ask the hardware man for wire cloth of 2 or 3 meshes to the inch. In the other end of box cut a hole about 3 x 6 inches near the top, and cover it with wire cloth also. Arrange a wooden door to close up this hole in very cold weather. Make the lid to fit tightly but so it can be easily raised or removed. Put a shelf lengthwise of the box 6 inches wide, 4 inches from floor. Have the shelf so it is readily removable when you wish to clean or inspect the hutch. In good weather such a hutch may be placed outside and a run made of wire cloth or of boards, so the pets may enjoy exercising in the open air and picking grass for themselves. But the hutch must be made entirely rain-proof, if it is to be left out in the damp weather. Keep the hutch in a light place when it is indoors. Put it near a window, where the sun will shine into it for as long a time each day as possible. In very hot weather the best location is in the shade, on the grass, in the open air.

A Small Caviary.

A small house of even 6 x 8 feet will accommodate a number of indoor hutches if they are made uniform in size so they can be piled up three or four high. Out-door hutches may be used the entire year in a back yard or elsewhere if no building or shed is available, but if they can be kept in a dry place in cold weather it is more convenient for the attendant.

Large Caviaries.

For raising cavies on a larger scale, buildings similar to poultry houses are commonly utilized. Any weather-tight building will do. One with a floor is best. With boards or wire netting fence off runs for each pen of cavies, and have a little door so that they may be shut in during the night and when the ground is wet. The fences need not be over 12 inches high, but must be fas-tened tightly to the ground so the animals cannot squeeze under. If dogs are likely to stray in the vicinity it will be necessary to have the outside fences high enough to keep them out. See that the runs are sheltered in part from the direct rays of the sun in hot weather. The pens should be provided with plenty of hay or straw for bedding, and in the winter weather should have boxes placed on top of the bedding for warm sleeping quar-ters. The boxes are turned bottom side up and have a doorway cut through one end. This little doorway is to be left open for ventilation at all times.

For Peruvians.

The Peruvian being a long-haired cavy, should have a hutch somewhat different from the short, smooth-haired cavies. The Peruvian requires more room, and care should be taken that there are no rough edges in the hutch which might damage its coat. The opening in the door should be large enough to remove the cavy without injuring it. The floor should be covered with clean sawdust, and the hay supplied for bedding should be cut into short lengths so the Peruvian cannot get its long coat entangled. These precautions need not be observed with other than exhibition Peruvians. Those which are used merely for breeding should have the hair clipped short enough so that it will not cause trouble. Peruvians are more susceptible to dampness than the short-haired cavies, as the long coats retain moisture for a longer time.

Protecting Outdoor Hutches.

If small hutches are to be left outside during severe weather they should be placed against a wall or in some place sheltered from the wind. You can further aid in retaining the heat by covering the hutch with bags or burlap or by piling hay over and around it, remembering at all times to leave a small opening at the door for ventilation.

Ventilation.

Ventilation is a subject poorly understood by the great majority of persons. We all know that the word means the process of replacing foul or vitiated air with fresh or pure air, but the processes we use are frequently not well adapted for the purpose intended, and often cause trouble for ourselves and for those animals dependent upon us and our "process" for their supply of oxygen and the conservation of their heat. In the first place, we should understand that a sleeping room, a stable or a hutch may be *cold* and yet not *ventilated* at all. Airtight walls thinly constructed of a material which is a good conductor of heat (metals are such materials) would cause such a condition. Now, clearly the remedy would be to make thicker walls of a different material, such as wood, and make an opening for the pasage of air. Air moves upwards when expelled from the lungs into a cold atmosphere, so that cold in a way assists ventilation by rapidly removing the vitiated air.

Now, in a hutch ventilation in cold weather is amply accomplished by a small opening in one end. The walls should be of wood, and may be supplemented to any extent by placing suitable materials, such as additional boards, hay, leaves, bags, rags or sawdust on the outside, but the one opening must be unobstructed. The opening should be about on a level with the heads of the animals, and in very cold weather should be approximately the size of a one-inch augur hole for each cavy. As the weather moderates, enlarge the opening slightly. In warm summer weather there should be openings in both ends of hutch; in fact, one end should be entirely open. Do not be afraid of draughts in dry, warm weather. On the other hand, do not shut off the air in case of rain; shut out the water only. In cold weather, when the openings are reduced in size, make sure that the hutch is clean. A filthy floor is especially dangerous when the air passages are small. The greater the number of cavies in a hutch the larger must your openings be and the less thickness is required in the walls.

Supply plenty of bedding in cold weather, particularly when the hutch contains only a few cavies. An abundance of bedding insures warmth and will not seriously interfere with ventilation.

Cleaning.

All pens and hutches must be kept clean by removing droppings and any wet or dirty bedding once a week. If your cavies are kept in clean, sanitary quarters, fed and watered properly, and not allowed to get wet, you may feel sure you will have no sickness or disease amongst them.

All hutches or housings should be rat proof. It is a common and mistaken idea that guinea pigs will kill rats. Guinea pigs are very similar in nature to rabbits, and rats are very fond of the young, though we have never known of rats killing full-grown guinea pigs.

TORTOISE AND WHITE CAVY.

CHAPTER VI.

PROFITS IN CAVIES.

There is at the present moment an unusual opportunity to make money by raising guinea pigs. There is no doubt of this. We are somewhat enthusiastic on the subject, and might be liable to overestimate the amount which can actually be made on the pretty little animals, and so, just to be on the safe side, we will take the figures as given by the United States Government after several years of experimenting with guinea pigs in the Bureau of Animal Industry. Their estimate of the possible profits is conservative—surely not exaggerated.

U. S. Government Says:

The Government Bulletin says: "The numerous inquiries received by the Department of Agriculture concerning proper methods of rearing guinea pigs or cavies show a widespread interest in the subject throughout the United States."

"The cost of rearing a guinea pig to maturity (age 4 or 5 months) at the department stations has been estimated by those in charge at from 50 to 60 cents. With their own labor, private breeders, especially farmers with plenty of green food at command, could probably reduce the cost by half."

"In medical research, especially in testing and standardizing antitoxins, immature animals, weighing 250 grams (nearly 9 ounces) are required. This weight is attained in about six weeks, and the cost of feeding the animals until suitable for this purpose will be correspondingly less. Guinea pigs sell at various prices, dependent on supply and demand. The average price for several years has been about 75 cents, but laboratories now report that suitable stock is scarce, and that they have been paying from $1.00 to $1.50 for their supply of animals."

And again: "A female in her breeding prime may be expected to raise about 12 to 15 young each year."

The Government report concludes: "The rearing of guinea pigs requires no extraordinary knowledge and no great outlay of capital. Little space is needed to accommodate the animals, which are hardy and easily managed. They make interesting pets and are useful food animals."

What the Government Figures Mean.

Taking the Government figures as a basis, let us count up just what the profits would be on, say, 100 Does and 25 Bucks in one year. The cost of rearing a cavy to "maturity is 50 to 60 cents," so we will count that it costs 20 cents to rear them to 9 ounces weight, the marketable size, and will estimate the cost of feeding the parent stock at $1.50 per year each. As the females "raise 12 to 15 young each year," we will take the mean of the two figures, which would be 13½. Likewise, taking the mean of "$1.00 to $1.50" gives us $1.25 each as the market value of our product.

```
Raising 1,350 young at 20c............  $270.00
Feeding 125 old cavies at $1.50........   187.50
Incidental expenses, estimated........   100.00
                                         -------
Total cost of 1,350 young.........        557.50

Value of 1,350 young at $1.25.......$1687.50
Cost of feeding young and old.......   557.50
                                       -------
Net profit for one year............$1130.00
```

If you do the work yourself and happen to have plenty of green food at command, you "could probably reduce the cost by half," and this would give you a profit on the little herd of 125 cavies of $1,358.75. This number would require but a few hours' attention each day. A man should be able to care for five times that number if he devoted all his time to them. By the same Government estimate, the net profit on 500 females and 125 males would be $5,650.00 per year, and if the cost of feeding and labor were reduced "by half," the 625 cavies would pay their owner $6,793.75 per year. These sums look big, but they are based on the Government figures, and the Government is hard-headed, cold-blooded and conservative when it gives figures on such matters.

Starting.

We would advise any one thinking of raising guinea pigs to start with a few and study them as their number increased. They will multiply quickly enough, and you will have time to arrange additional quarters for them as required. True, no extraordinary knowledge is required, but we would not like to see 500 cavies purchased by one who has had no experience, and who most likely would not have prepared suitable pens, and perhaps no supply of proper food. By starting with only a few, there is little invested and consequently little risked.

In raising guinea pigs there is always the assurance that no disease will sweep away all the profits, if the stock is properly fed and kept in clean quarters.

Other Markets.

As big as the foregoing figures are, there is a way of selling cavies which brings a much greater return per head. The Government has based its estimates of the

A FINE SPECIMEN OF PERUVIAN (LONG HAIRED) CAVY.

market value upon the prices paid by laboratories. We know of several Guinea Pig farms, one large one in particular, where practically the entire output is sold for breeding purposes. The prices are never less than $3.00 per pair, and for the fancy stock they get from $4.00 to $12.00 per pair, and sometimes more. Of course, this does not include the finest specimens. They recently refused $100.00 for a pair of prize-winning Peruvians.

The demand for cavies for breeding purposes will undoubtedly continue to increase for many years, and those who start now in the business of raising them will reap a rich harvest.

CHAPTER VII.

GUINEA PIGS (CAVIES) AS PETS.

Cavies make ideal pets. They are intelligent, clean and pretty. They do not bite or scratch. They may be trained to do any number of tricks. The young ones are well developed when born, have their eyes open, are fully furred, lively and "cute." They are not as common as cats, dogs, rabbits, etc., and they require less space and less feed. They are more of a novelty, more interesting to ourselves and our friends. Then, too, there is always that opportunity for *profit*.

The Cavy's Voice.

The cavy frequently becomes much attached to its owner and very affectionate. It has a peculiar and varied cry, sometimes like a whistle, and expresses gladness or affection, fear and pain. When frightened it sometimes makes a very peculiar chattering sound, a sound of fear or defiance.

The length of life of the cavy is not known to any certainty. It appears that no one has given the subject of its longevity any thought but there are reports of cavies living to the age of 8 or 10 years.

As a Hobby.

As a hobby, cavy keeping offers many inducements, one of which is the small space required by the animals. Then too, the cost of purchasing and maintaining them is so small that they are easily within the reach of all. And above all they are healthy little fellows and do not require much time in caring for them and the services of the veterinarian are never required. A fact which will be appreciated by those who have previously kept dogs or cats is that no meat of any kind enters into the cavy's diet. You can lay in as large a stock of feed as you like; it will keep.

Cavy Shows.

In England the cavy has become very popular, and special cavy shows are held there at which valuable prizes are given for those approaching nearest to the standard of perfection. The prize winners are always in great demand and readily sell for £5 to £25 ($25 to $125.) There are in this country as yet no shows devoted entirely to cavies but in all of the important poultry shows there are departments devoted to cavies and prizes are awarded. The breeding of fancy stock is rapidly increasing and at no distant time we may expect the cavy exhibits to be equally or more interesting than the poultry, though the numbers shown may be less. At the present time the beginner has a good chance to win in the cavy shows because there are no old breeders in this country and as a rule the specimens shown are far from the standard. At present we are all pioneers.

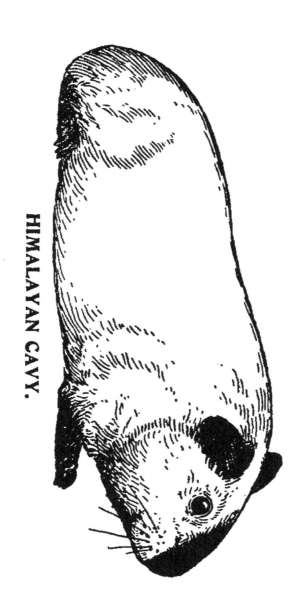

HIMALAYAN CAVY.

CHAPTER VIII.

CAVIES OR GUINEA PIGS AS FOOD.

At the present time cavies are not much used for food in the United States. This is natural as there are no cavies for sale in the markets and if they were offered for sale the people would not know what they were. All that is needed to make the cavy as popular as the chicken is education along that line and the Government has already begun the work.

We may expect in a few years to see cavies dressed and for sale in all the markets where meats and poultry are sold. The cavy, when properly cooked, is delicious, wholesome and nourishing. It is a clean animal, certainly much cleaner than any chicken; it can be raised largely on grass and other cheap foods easily obtainable. It is most easily managed and cared for, all of which goes to make a pound of cavy cost less to produce than a pound of chicken. But it is not its low cost which is its greatest recommendation but its high quality, its delicious flavor. In South America cavies are considered good game and are much hunted.

Killing.

In preparing the cavy for cooking the neck is broken by striking its head with the side of the hand while the animal is suspended by the hind legs, then it is bled by cutting the throat with a knife. A string about a foot long is tied, one end to each hind leg and looped over a hook or nail in a convenient post or wall and the animal is skinned in the same way as a rabbit or squirrel would be; that is, a cut is made in the skin along each hind leg and continued across from the one cut to the other and by pulling the skin apart at the cut, the legs are bared, the ends then cut from the hocks and the skin removed with as little trouble, and in much the same manner as a boy removes his shirt when he goes in swimming.

The old Guinea Pig books say the animal is very difficult to skin and should be "scalded and scraped like a pig." Apparently the authors never saw one skinned. We have skinned rabbits, squirrels, sheep, cows, deer, antelopes, minks, muskrats, skunks, 'coons 'possums and a few other animals including even cats and dogs but the cavy is the quickest and easiest of them all.

Any practical cook will know many ways in which to cook the cavy, but as suggestions we will add a few recipes:

Brown Soup.

Place a large fat cavy in two quarts of water, with vegetables, a middling-sized onion, cut into rings and fried brown, pepper and salt to taste, a small blade of mace, and two tablespoonfuls of mushroom ketchup. Stew for four or five hours over a brisk fire, keeping the quantity of soup up to two quarts by adding boiling water occasionally. Strain the stock through a wire sieve, and thicken it with a brown roux. Have ready the best joints of two small cavies. Stew these very gently in the thickened stock until quite tender. The flavor may have diminished in the long cooking, and some more seasoning may require to be added. Serve very hot, with fried toast, cut in dice.

Stewed Cavy.

Two nice young cavies, one quart of milk, one table-spoonful of flour, a blade of mace, salt and pepper. Mix the flour into a smooth paste with one half glass of milk; then add the rest of the milk, cut the cavy up into convenient pieces, place in a stew-pan with the other ingredients, and simmer gently until perfectly tender.

Cavy a l'Italienne.

Cut a cavy in pieces, wash in cold water, a little salt-ed. rrepare in a stew pan some flour and butter; stir until brown. Then put in the pieces of cavy and keep stirring and turning until they are tinged with a little color. Then add six small onions not cut up, some pieces of carrot, potato and about a pint of soup stock. Bring to a boil and let simmer until tender. Serve all to-gether in a deep dish.

Pot Pie a la Coqueta.

Two cavies, one-fourth pound fat pork, four eggs, pepper, butter, a little powdered mace, a few drops of lemon-juice, puff-paste. Cut a pair of cavies into ten pieces, soak in salt and water half an hour, and simmer until half done, in enough water to cover them. Cut a quarter of a pound of pork into slices, and boil four eggs hard. Lay some pieces of pork in the bottom of the dish, the next a layer of cavy. Upon this spread slices of boiled egg and pepper and butter. Sprinkle, more-over, with a little powdered mace, a few drops of lemon-juice upon each piece of meat. Proceed in this manner until the dish is full, the top layer being pork. Pour in water in which the cavy was boiled; when you have salted it and added a few lumps of butter in flour, cover with puff-paste, make a hole in the middle and bake for an hour. Cover with paper if it should boil too fast.

Curried Cavy.

One cavy, one-fourth pound of butter, one apple, two onions, two tablespoonfuls curry-powder, one-fourth pint of cream, one pint stock, one lemon, a salt-spoonful of salt. Melt butter over the fire, peel and chop the onions as fine as possible, then put them into the melted butter to fry a light brown. After the cavy has been properly prepared for cooking, wash well and dry in a cloth, cut in pieces of equal size. After straining the butter from the onions, return the former to the stew-pan, put in pieces of cavy and allow to fry for 10 or 15 minutes, turning occasionally. Peel and core the apples, and chop as fine as possible. When the meat is done add to it two tablespoonfuls of curry-powder and the salt, stirring for five minutes, then add the fried onion, chopped apple, and a pint of good stock. Allow to simmer for two hours, at the end of the time add the cream, squeeze the juice from the lemon into stew-pan. It is then ready to serve.

Cavy aux Fine Herbs.

Take a full grown and fat hog cavy. killed and cleaned as previously described. Blanch it in one pint of boiling water, cut it into joints; make the water thick with a white roux of butter and flour. Put it over the fire in a moderate-sizeu stew-pan; stirr till thick and quite smooth; add one tablespoonful of parsley and one of green onions chopped small, and pepper and salt to taste; stew the cavy in this for two hours or until it is perfectly tender. If a pint of stock be used instead of the water, this dish will be much improved; thicken with the yoke of an egg and serve.

Cavy en Gibelotte.

The cavy should be cut into joints, something as a cooked rabbit is carved. The body will cut into 4 or

5 pieces. Procure a middle-sized eel, and, having prepared it in the usual way, cut it into lengths of two inches. Make a *roux* with flour and butter. *Sautez* the cavy and eel in this, with the addition of mushrooms and little onions; moisten with white wine or vinegar and double the quantity of stock; season with pepper, salt, a bouquet of parsley, thyme, and a little green onion. Then take out the pieces of eel and the little onions. Cook the cavy fast (*a grand feu*) until the sauce is reduced to two-thirds; replace the eel and little onions, and finish the cooking slowly (*a feu doux.*) If there be any fat in the sauce, take it off. Take out the bouquet, and serve very hot.

Jellied Cavy.

Two cavies, one ounce of butter, pepper and salt, one-half packet of gelatin. Boil the cavy until the water is reduced to a pint; pick the meat from the bones in fair-sized pieces, removing all gristle and bone. Skim the fat from the liquor, add an ounce of butter, a little pepper and salt, and half a packet of gelatin. Put the cut-up cavy into a mould, wet with cold water; when the gelatin has dissolved, pour the liquor hot over the cavy. Turn out when cold.

CHAPTER IX.

CAVY FUR.

Most kinds of furs are steadily getting scarcer and higher in price. Cavy fur has never been used extensively but it is a fur of fairly good quality, especially the Peruvian or long-haired variety and we see no reason why it should not be used extensively when there is enough of it. It can be bred in almost any color and the red is different from any fur on the market.

Contrary to the general idea, the cavy is easily skinned and should always be so treated when preparing for food.

In order that the fur shall be of good quality it is necessary that the animal be killed when the fur is at its best, that is, when the animal is not shedding. This can be ascertained by rubbing or pulling the fur before killing. The fur is usually at its best in the winter season and the fur of the young animals is considered better than that of the old cavies. The more desirable colors would be black, white, red or grey.

Curing Skins.

Stretch the fresh skin tightly on a board and tack it, with flesh side out. Scrape off any meat or fat, being careful not to cut the skin. Put 10 ounces of alum and one-half ounce of salt in a half pint of hot water. Then apply this solution while warm to the skin with a cloth or sponge, three or four times a day, until the skin is thoroughly dry. This will take three or four days. The skin may now be removed from the board and worked with the hands until the skin is soft and pliable. A very little Neat's Foot Oil may be applied to skin on the flesh side to aid in softening it.

CHAPTER X.

DISEASES.

A chapter on the Diseases of Cavies seems almost superfluous in view of the fact that cavies are so rarely attacked by disease and then only when badly treated. Proper care is a positive preventive. On the other hand people do not and will not always give the animals the common and necessary care. Hence, we sometimes find cavies in need of medical treatment or more properly in need of dietary or hygienic attention. The cavy's ailments are always caused by overcrowding, draftiness, filthiness, dampness, carelessness in feeding or some kindred reason.

Constipation.

This trouble is usually caused by a lack of green food and the remedy is obvious. You may give one-half teaspoonful of olive oil or 10 drops of molasses in a teaspoonful of milk, but these remedies will probably not be needed if green food can be had. If you discover a case of constipation begin by feeding some fresh apple daily and the trouble will most likely disappear.

Dropsy.

A form of this disease is sometimes found to affect cavies and the cause is usually a lack of green food or it may be that dampness or draftiness has caused the animal to take cold. A cure can usually be affected by removing the cause. If the animal is a valuable one, remove it to a clean dry warm hutch, give proper dry and green foods, plenty of pure water and some bread and milk.

Scours (Diarrhea).

This sometimes occurs where too little dry food and too much, or the wrong kind of green food has been

DISEASES

given. Frequently caused by an excess of some green food to which the animal has not been accustomed. When you begin feeding something new, introduce it sparingly and gradually increase the portion fed.

Parturition.

Does sometimes die from trouble at this time either before or after giving birth to young. The trouble may be caused by fatness or the reverse, a poorly nourished condition or from severely cold weather and a drafty hutch. Overcrowding may cause it also.

Premature Birth.

May be caused by fright, overfatness or by physical weakness. Weakness and the consequent premature birth are often caused by permitting the female to breed too often. Some breeders say that two litters a year are all that a female should be allowed. Others say three a year. There is, and indeed can be, no rule as to this. A Doe well fed, well cared for and supplied with plenty of clean water will produce four litters a year and apparently suffer no ill effects, whereas another Doe not so well treated would not be able to produce even three litters in the same time, without being overtaxed.

Lice.

Cavies have been known to become infested with vermin but such a condition would not speak well for the attendant as it occurs only when filth is allowed to accumulate. The remedy is first to clean out the hutch and furnish a bedding of sawdust with which has been mixed a small quantity of Persian Insect Powder. Some of the powder may also be rubbed into the fur.

Rats and Mice.

These should be exterminated or shut out of the caviary as they spread filth and disease and at least eat food intended for the cavies. Rats frequently kill and eat young cavies.

Clarke's Great Book on Canaries.

CANARY BREEDING

A Condensed Treatise on the

Breeding, Feeding and Training of

SINGING CANARIES

Tells about the varieties bred in different countries and which are the **Best Varieties** How to select stock and cages. Where to locate the cage. Foods and supplies. Destroying insects. Mating, Quarreling, Kissing, Marrying, Nest Building and materials Proper diet for birds when breeding and no breeding. All about the handling of eggs Hatching, etc. How to distinguish the sexes Training to sing.

Possible troubles and How to Avoid Them Soft shell eggs, Egg eating. Feeding young Sweating females, German Secret for coloring and a chapter on Diseases with Home Treatment.

PRICE 10 CENTS

Send five 2c stamps or a silver dime.

DUNLAP-CLARKE CO.
Chatham. N. Y. or 100 Fifth Avenue, New York City.

Printed in Great Britain
by Amazon

41749327R00033